Written and performed by

Clementine Bogg-Hargroves

Published by Playdead Press 2022

© Clementine Bogg-Hargroves 2022

Clementine Bogg-Hargroves has asserted her rights under the Copyright, Design and Patents Act, 1988, to be identified as the author of this work.

A CIP catalogue record for this book is available from the British Library.

ISBN 978-1-910067-99-4

Caution
All rights whatsoever in this play including readings and excerpts are strictly reserved and application for performance should be sought through Mark Ashmore via markashmorefrsa@gmail.com before rehearsals begin. No performance may be given unless a license has been obtained.

This book is sold subject to the condition that it shall not by way of trade or otherwise, be lent, re-sold, hired out, or otherwise circulated without the publisher's prior consent in any form of binding or cover other than that in which it is published and without a similar condition including this condition being imposed on the subsequent purchaser.

Playdead Press
www.playdeadpress.com

To Lewis Coleman and Zoey Barnes.

Written and performed by
Clementine Bogg-Hargroves

CREATIVES:

Director & Dramaturg	Zoey Barnes
Producer	Mark Ashmore
Sound Designer	George Roberts
Set Designers	Timothy Hargroves & Paul Coleman
Stage Manager	Adam Jefferys
PR	Madelaine Bennet

The following script is the version that was performed at The Pleasance during the Edinburgh Fringe Festival in 2021.

Clementine Bogg-Hargroves | Writer and Performer
Clem started to seriously pursue acting after graduating with an MA Hons in Arabic from The University of Edinburgh. She went back home to North Yorkshire, where she produced and acted in *Constellations* by Nick Payne and *Spine* by Clara Brennan, as well as appearing in the annual Skipton Christmas pantomimes. Wanting to level up her skills, Clem went to drama school. This is where she met her partner Lewis Coleman, with whom she created the production company Get Giddier, and *SKANK*'s Director, Zoey Barnes.

SKANK is Clem's first full-length play, it started its journey as a 90 minutes piece in a packed out cafe in Skipton, and over the course of two years slowly made its way to the Edinburgh Fringe 2021.

Clem is currently working on her next piece, *Gabby*, as well as adapting *SKANK* for TV.

For further credits please see www.getgiddier.com

Zoey Barnes | Director and Dramaturg
Zoey has a First Class BA in Drama and met Clem whilst they did their MA in Professional Acting. The two took Zoey's play *Austen Power* to the Edinburgh Free Fringe and started working on *SKANK* in 2019. Over the course of a few intense weekends in a Quaker's cottage in Skipton, Zoey supported Clem in the making of the play. The two have a magical, telepathic working relationship and make each other wee with laughter, which hopefully is evident in *SKANK*. Outside of that, Zoey has directed various short pieces. She is also an actor and sews up a storm in her home atelier.

Further directing credits: *Sirens* (King's Arms, Salford), and short plays for Manchester ADP and Bluestocking Theatre.

Costume credits: *A Midsummer Night's Dream* and *Vagina Cake* (HER Productions), *Jekyll and Hyde* (Box Clever Theatre).

Acting credits: Laertes, *Hamlet* (HER Productions), Vanity, *Mother Goose* (Trinity Arts Centre), Leia, *Purge* (The Lowry) Queen, *Knowledge and a Girl* (C Venues, Edinburgh).

Mark Ashmore | Producer
Mark graduated in 2005 from Northbrook with a First Class Honours in Theatre Arts. At the time of writing, he is a final year PhD researcher in the school of Mathematics and Computer Science at Liverpool John Moore's University, hoping to attain a doctorate in Immersive Arts.

Past credits include: Director of *The Lost Generation* (Feature Film), Director of *Portal (Online Series)*, Virtual Reality Director and Producer for *Lookout* (BBC, VR Project), as well as *SKANK*, *Gabby* and *Four To The Floor* as Producer.

Mark is the CEO of Future Artists, an arts collective working with creatives in the fields of film, theatre and Immersive events to push each respective medium.

The company's missions statement: "Without deviation from the norm, progress is not possible." – Frank Zappa.

Dream it, then find the people to make it happen.

More at www.futureartists.net

George Roberts | Sound Designer
George is a sound technician/musician/tech wizard from South Manchester. He has a degree in Creative Music Technology from The University of Huddersfield, and has been flexing his audio-muscles for the past decade in any project he can get his ears on. These recently include a VR exhibition for the BBC, working on set with the Get Giddier film collective, and playing keyboards in his band Legs on Wheels (they are currently working on their debut album). He's been part of the *SKANK* since 2019 and has probably seen the play more than anyone else on the planet.

Adam Jefferys | Stage Manager
Adam is a Theatre Technician and Actor, having trained at East 15 Acting School and Royal Central School of Speech and Drama.

Recent production credits include: *Project Dictator* (New Diorama Theatre), *The Musical That Goes Right* (Cockpit), *Dorian* (Reading Rep), *Drag Queens VS Zombies* (Pleasance Theatre), *Dog Show* (Pleasance Theatre) and *Robin Hood* (Harlow Playhouse). Performance Credits: *Small Town, Big Hell* (Short Film); *Protest* (Short Film); *uwantme2killhim?* (Feature Film); *Wild Bill* (Feature Film); *Wireless Operator* (Theatre).

About Future Artists
Future Artists, founded in Manchester by Mark Ashmore in 2009, is the arts collective and company which has supported the development of *SKANK* since 2019. Over the course of a decade, Future Artists has morphed into a film, events, and theatre producing company. The company aims to support northern-based artists by nurturing new and original voices, as well as backing original and innovative ideas.

Acknowledgements

David Roberts, owner of Hettie's Cafe where SKANK made its debut, without your trust none of this would have been possible.

Lucy Arditti, for reading the first draft and for your concise, constructive and kind feedback.

Jayne Turner, Sophie Todd and Alison Coleman for your unending belief and support.

Skipton's knitting elite for the inspiration and the stoic ticket purchasing.

Steve Charlton, for lending your voice to Dr. Twigden.

Harry Stachini, for being an all-round great human and for 'Biscuit Brigade'.

Leah Sherrington, for letting us turn your beautiful studio into a SKANK rehearsal space whenever needed.

Liam Rigby, for the incredible SKANK photos over the years, the love and support and the never-ending supply of quotes.

Paul Coleman, for your unquestioned support and your DIY prowess.

Mum and Dad, for always supporting me in my varied schemes over the years, for your far-and-wide ranging skills that I can always rely on, and for everything else. I love you.

With special thanks to Lewis Coleman, for your devising and writing contributions, for your patience and generosity, and for your unwavering and constant support. Thank-you.

Notes on the text

Other characters can be recorded voices, played by other actors or played by Kate.

A (/) indicates someone being cut off.

Pauses and beats are indicated by the space given between lines.

Notes on the set

The original productions of SKANK used a table, 2 chairs, laptop and, of course, a bean can as set. The table was turned into a gynaecological table through the attachment of two stirrups with a pulley system to one edge of the table and a roll of medical tissue paper to the other.

Any companies wishing to tour this work are free to tackle the problem in their own way, whether it be similarly DIY-esque or simply physicalising the use of stirrups.

The original production played a high-pitched ringing sound into the auditorium to indicate Kate's tinnitus at key moments of the play.

work porn

Monday. The recycling bins haven't been delivered. **Kate** *goes to find* **Karen,** *the Office Administrator, with an empty bean can in her hand.* **Karen** *is from Barnsley.*

KATE:	Karen the recycling bins haven't arrived.
KAREN:	You're joking!
KATE:	No.
KAREN:	Well, I tell ya what love, it were a reet nightmare! I know it's hard to believe Kate but I went and forgot me login! I'm a thick bitch. So I clicks forgot me password and a little quiz popped up in a 4 by 4 grid! Tiles! Select all the traffic cones it said! You know me Kate, I'm not one to shy away from a battle o'wit! I beat it's quiz and with all t'excitement I forgot what colour bin thou wanted! So I just got a black one coz black goes wi'owt dun't it?
KATE:	Yeah.
KAREN:	It does.
KATE:	Yeah.
KAREN:	Dun't it?
KATE:	Yes. But that's not a recycling bin Karen, it's just for general waste.
KAREN:	You're joking. I tell thee what I should be put in that bloody waste bin! I'm a shit.

KATE: *(taken aback slightly)* ... You know what, send me the login and I'll sort it.

Kate goes to her desk and logs on to her computer, she notices that her schedule has been updated. She's not pleased.

KATE: They've put me on an early lunch again! All next week. 12 o'clock lunch. That means that when I come back from my lunch I've still got 4 units left until I can go home, instead of 3. I break down my time into units when I'm here, in the office, to make it more... manageable. You probably do the same thing, right?

There's a hierarchy in this office, and yours truly is just one above the bottom rung. Which is a bit rich considering I've got a Scottish masters degree. But no-one gives a shit about that.

What this really boils down to though is a power struggle. Between me and them: the scheduling team. Or as I like to call them, The Biscuit Brigade! Anyway, I've got my heart set on that 1pm lunch slot, and you better believe that I'm gonna get it. I just need to target the weakest link in the old Fox's Cream Crunch crew and bend them to my will.

Okay so who've we got? David. Rich Tea. He gives off a weak vibe. He's got that double-chin on a skinny person thing going on. Oh shit, forgot about Lisa. Bourbon Cream. He's got Lisa at his side to protect him from my charms, and no matter how hard I think I am she'd flatten me before I got the chance to slip David a WHSmith voucher. Alright then, it's going to have to be Annie. Fig roll. Anal Annie. Right. Compliments for Annie. Compliments for Annie. Compliments. 'Annie! Wow! I absolutely love your...' nope. Got nothing.

Could just seduce her? I think she'd go for it. I bet she's filthy. Secretly into all that chaining up stuff. Whipping. Leather. More whipping. Yeah. That's classic Annie. But, what if she wants a relationship? I'd be closing off any potential romantic avenues with sexy Gary. Unless that'd lure him in more?

Regardless of Sexy Gary's interest in threesomes, this whole plan seems to be pointing towards me getting it on with Anal Annie in order to secure a late lunch.

Worth it.

Kate *heads back to her desk and sits down in front of her computer.*

Should probably do some work.

Kate *starts to do something that looks like she's working. She keeps checking in with her new friends (the audience), making 'Eugh I can't be bothered' faces.*
Her facetious facade begins to drop as her anxiety begins to kick in. She tries to distract herself.

This is really boring though!

During this next section **Kate** *is getting distracted by tinnitus (constant high pitched ringing) in her right ear. She starts to feel the weight of her boredom, her tinnitus is getting louder, she feels her anxiety swirl around her tummy.*

I mean, what am I even doing here? Wasn't I supposed to be famous and successful by now? Is this it? If this is it, I might as well give up on any hopes and dreams.

Kate *snaps out of it. The tinnitus stops.*
She sees **Linda** *at the other end of the office.*

She seems okay, Linda. She's looking really good at the moment. Maybe I should go to the gym. Could go to that Body Attack class where all the perfect people go. The thought of it makes me want to cry into an eclair.

They say exercise helps anxiety and depression don't they? Fuck off.

Linda's in a relationship with IT Tony. I sometimes picture them having sex. I bet he wears his cycling helmet. Tour de France groupie. I tell you what, if I have to hear another story about them accidentally buying matching lycra shorts, I might have to frame him for paedophilia. Oh Christ here she comes.

LINDA:	Kate!
KATE:	Linda! Hey!
LINDA:	Lovely day isn't it! Could you believe the traffic coming in?! I thought I was going to be late. Anyway, crisis averted! Oh what's this little fella doing here? *(referring to the bean can)* Do you want me to get rid of it for you?
KATE:	Oh no thanks, I'm trying to recyc/
LINDA:	Awww! That's great Kate. Well done you! Right well, let's get caffeinated! AM I RIGHT?! Honestly I come out with some random things! Must be all those sudokus. Oh dear! I'm going to have a stroke! Oh stop it Kate! Oh my heart! We have fun don't we! I think I'm in need of some refreshment! Can I get you anything?

KATE:	How about a will to live?
LINDA:	Oh honestly you are so funny Kate! Witty! You are very witty aren't you. We should get together! Me, you, Tony, and... a hot date... for me! No, no, no - obviously for you because I'm engaged to Tony.
KATE:	Yeah I know you are.
LINDA:	*(as she leaves)* Oh bloody nora I'm getting a sweat on. Anyway, can't be standing here and having fun all day can I? I better run chica, but I'll catch you later and we'll get this date organised!
KATE:	Definitely! *(she watches* **Linda** *walk away)* Just look at her. I wish I was like her. Simple. That's the thing isn't it, when you're smart it's harder to be happy because you just know more. Guaranteed I'd be happy if my primary concern was the weather forecast. She'll probably go home tonight and have some... grilled chicken, with a side of steamed leeks, and treat herself to a rolo yoghurt from Asda. To be fair, those rolo yoghurts – they're unreal.

Kate *spots* **Sexy Gary.**

Sexy Gary! Okay, look intelligent. And sexy. *(She starts to tap the keyboard)* And type, type, type, type; index finger lightly

	brushing the mouth, slightly part the lips, and… look up. Gary!? So weird to see you here!
SEXY GARY:	Erm, I work here.
KATE:	Right! Duh!
SEXY GARY:	Yeah. I better go anyway.
KATE:	No wait! I mean, tell me about it. I'm snowed-under over here! What are they trying to do, bore us to death?!

Kate *is thinking how she can retain his attention. She starts to act out ways in which one could die - hanging, shot in the head, whatever you fancy.*

> Chance'd be a fine thing!

Sexy Gary *is walking away.*

> Alright yeah, fair enough. I better get back to it as well so, catch ya later skater!
> Nailed it.
> …
>
> I could check to see if they've blocked porn on the computer.

Kate *types pornhub on the laptop and presses enter. Porn noises start. Loudly. She furiously tries to click it off, it won't stop so she slams the laptop shut. Porn noises stop.*

> I'm in between jobs at the moment.

Well I've got a 'job'. But it's not my real 'job', if you know what I mean. I mean it is my 'job' but it's not my occupation. It's not what I 'do'. I just have to do it so that I can live.

I've been a temp at this office for about a month now and today I am getting my monthly review. I don't exactly know what they'll be reviewing because it's not like I do anything. My job is so pointless that instead of doing whatever it is that I'm supposed to be doing, I managed to read *Revolutionary Road*, cover to cover, over 2 days, and nobody noticed.

I applied for a temporary office administrator role. I thought that that would involve some emailing, maybe a few coffee runs and the occasional minute taking in meetings. You know, not so much that I break a sweat, but with enough variety and activities to stave me away from the fifth floor window.
I don't know what the rest of them do all day but they seem to be really busy. Stressed almost. With what exactly... I don't know. It's odd. For me, it's the opposite. It's when I think about life

beyond menial jobs that I feel like I'm going to shit my pants in pure panic. Surely other people feel like this, but nobody is talking about it so we're all just walking around the planet holding it in. Anyway, so when I'm in the office it's like a holiday for my brain because I don't feel anything about anything that happens in there.

I change jobs a lot. One of my favourite things to do when looking for work is calculating how much money I could save if I stayed there for a whole year. Then I'd have a bit of money behind me to pursue what I actually want to do. Which is writing. I think. I'll probably be shit and that could be why I haven't done anything about it yet. So I guess this means I'll be staying here. Until I quit. Again.

BOSS: Kate, would you mind coming into my office for a minute.

KATE: Oh yeah sure Chris. That's my boss. I wonder what he…
Oh god. He knows about the porn.

Boss's *office. There is a pause,* **Kate** *assumes she's about to be bollocked.*

KATE: Okay look Chris, I know that what I did is really inappropriate and unprofessional, and I want to take this opportunity to apologise and to promise that it won't happen again. I'm not even into whatever that was, I don't even know what you'd call that or how you'd search for it. I guess maybe, if you typed in... hamster... relief, that could work but...

BOSS: Hamster relief?

KATE: I mean that's probably not the 'title', it's just a description, but that's what I'm saying I don't even know what it's called so I couldn't have actively searched for - that.

BOSS: Kate, what are you talking about?

Kate *realises that* **Boss** *isn't talking about the porn.*

KATE: Gotcha! Oh you really fell for that one didn't Boss!

BOSS: Oh! I should've bloody known! That was a really great one as well! You little scamp!

KATE: Yeah... What did you want to talk to me about?

BOSS: I like it Kate! Straight back to business! Let's change gear for a moment. Well, I don't know if you know this but Linda has taken up the offer to work in HR. Ipso facto, we're left without a Production & Logistics Coordinator and Linda has put you forward for the position!

KATE:	I quit.
BOSS:	Oh… right…
	…
KATE:	Gotcha. Again.
BOSS:	Oh you are on fire today Kate! I didn't even know that was another joke! Touché! Brilliant.
KATE:	Yeah. But no of course I'll, I'll take the promotion Chris. Thank you. Thank you so much.
BOSS:	That is great news Kate! Just think of that extra fifty pounds per year in the old pension pot, ey! Every little helps! And as you are now a permanent member of staff, drum roll please…

There is a pause, **Boss** *is waiting for* **Kate** *to drum roll. She realises this and drum rolls.*

BOSS:	Free coffee from the posh machine!
KATE:	Free coffee! Wow! Yeah, that's great! … Great.
BOSS:	Lattes. Mmm…
KATE:	Mm.
BOSS:	MMMMMMmmmm!

Kate *acknowledges the latte love and starts to leave* **Boss's** *office.*

BOSS:	Oh I almost forgot! You're funny aren't you Kate?
KATE:	Oh well I don't know about that…

BOSS: The company have put together a little writing competition.

KATE: A writing competition?

BOSS: Yes, so let me see here. Okay so it has to be a story based in the office, any department, any department you like but it has to be funny. And the winner gets an extra week holiday! I might give it a bloody bash!

KATE: Oh wow thanks for that Chris, I'll definitely look into it.

café

KATE: Well I'm obviously going to win it. I haven't written anything yet but there's definitely something brewing up there *(indicating her brain)*. Definitely.

There's this very cool café-bar place called 'semicolon'. I know, awful isn't it. A lot of freelancers go there when they want to feel like they're doing work as opposed to spending all day at home battling the urge to wank every time they open their laptop.

But to be honest, we're all just looking at sex toys anyway. So the only thing we've achieved is the replacement of actual wanking with the planning of future wanking.

Kate *starts to get a bit anxious, her tinnitus is getting louder/she's noticing it more. She feels claustrophobic.*

Coming in here usually makes me sweat. I find it a bit stressful to be honest. Like, I want to write. I really want to write. But I just get distracted by things. Things that could go wrong. Bad things, with me, with

> my body. And then this constant, incessant, fucking ringing.

Kate *snaps herself out of it. The tinnitus stops.*

> But now I have an actual writing assignment so it should be easier. I have a focus. Funny piece about the office. You never know, could lead somewhere.
>
> Right! Let's get this show on the road!

Kate *opens her laptop and the porn noises start up again. She panic clicks and manages to shut them off. She mouths 'sorry' to a fellow café-goer. She notices she's brought the bean can with her and gets the attention of a waitress.*

KATE:	Excuse me, sorry? Hello? Hi. Do you have anywhere where I can recycle this please?
WAITRESS:	Not really. *(she leaves)*
KATE:	Alrighty.

Kate *goes back to trying to write.*

> All I can think about is sex. And that didn't help. I'm just staring at that tiny black cursor, slowly becoming turned on...

Cocky bastard *has come over to* **Kate**'s *table, he is looking at her smiling but not saying anything.*

KATE:	Yes?
COCKY BASTARD:	Hey.
KATE:	Hey.

Cocky bastard *doesn't reply. Continues to stare and smile like the cocky bastard he is.*

KATE:	Can I help you?
COCKY BASTARD:	Can I get you another… flat white is it? I know my coffee.
KATE:	It's an Americano. No I'm alright thanks, I've already had two.
COCKY BASTARD:	Nonsense. I'll get you another. We'll make it decaf. I'll have one too.
KATE:	I'd rather you didn't.
COCKY BASTARD:	But why not? It's free.
KATE:	Because I am very busy.
	I like the attention though. And it transpires that he is a 'semicolon' regular. We've had the odd conversation here and there. He's a freelance brand-designer. His working day involves going to cool restaurants, cafes, bars; asking for the manager and telling them that their website is shit and that he could make them a lot more money. He's that much of an arrogant little prick that people just go, "Yeah alright!" And then he sends them an invoice worth a

trillion pounds for a logo that is essentially the company name in comic sans.

Regardless, these flirty little chats have subsided into a deafening silence. He seems to have forgotten that I exist. Which I think is a bit fucking rich considering he's the one that was all 'Another?'. There was frisson. You can't mistake a bit of frisson can you? It's like *(***Kate** *demonstrates frisson)*.

Kate *looks back at Ann Summers on her laptop.*

Even a fresh batch of anal beads can't cheer me up.

Lunchtime. A group of hikers come into the café. I'm sat on a table for four. There's four of them. The only other table available is a table for two. It's awkward. I'm suddenly finding the blank document in front of me incredibly interesting. I can hear the ring leader of the group (purple bandana, blue waterproof trousers, offensively comfortable shoes) loudly point out that they won't be able to fit on the last remaining table. The rest of the gaggle encourages her with disappointed noises. FUCK.OFF. I just need to ride out these last few seconds of total social agony... But then, there's a fun little development. Cocky Bastard sidles up next to me. He asks: 'Do you live near here?', I reply, '6 and a half minutes' walk, 3 minutes jog.' He whispers, 'Shall we?'... Oh yeah.

Apparently he hates hikers as much as I do.

So you know... we had a little, you know. A little. I mean, a lady doesn't like to kiss and tell. But you know. We... *(does finger gesture for having sex)*. I've said too much! But! Seriously, it was... it was... I mean... Actually it wasn't that great. He did this thing where he, naked, crouched down above me and gently popped his balls on my chin. And then one of them kinda... fell off. And so the skin, the ballsack skin, stretched over my skin like a rookie skingraft. And his pubes formed this cute little sparse... beard... Anyway! I managed to finish the piece for the office! Turns out all I needed was a bit of semen for that inspirational boost. I actually wrote it. All 10 pages of it.

doctors

Kate *is at the reception desk for the doctors, out of breath, she's been running. Bean Can in her hand.*

KATE:	Hello, Kate Sharmack - I've got an appointment with/
RECEPTIONIST:	You're late.
KATE:	Oh, sorry about that. I was dropping off my aunt at the backgammon club so... shall I take a seat?
RECEPTIONIST:	Go straight through please. You're in room 6 with Doctor Magdalane Sniadek.
KATE:	Thank-you.
	What a bitch.

Kate *finds Room 6.*

KATE:	Hello/
DR MAGDA:	Wait.

Dr Magda *is typing up notes very loudly on her computer while* **Kate**, *not quite sure whether she should stay or leave, awkwardly stands and waits until she's finished.*

DR MAGDA:	*(finishes typing)* Yes. Hello Kate, so we're doing your smear test today?

Kate *doesn't have time to respond.*

DR MAGDA: Okay. So. If you'd like to take off your pants and sit up on here please. You can leave your can or bring it in with you. As you wish.

Kate *wraps a sheet of medical tissue paper around her bottom half and puts her legs into the stirrups. She grabs the bean can.*

DR MAGDA:	Have you had your smear test before?
KATE:	No. To be honest the idea of knowing what's going on inside my body is terrifying to me.
DR MAGDA:	Okay. I am going to do the smear for you now?
KATE:	Yes please. Thank-you.
DR MAGDA:	Kate I'm going to go in now, you might feel a slightly uncomfortable sensation but just try to relax.
KATE:	Alright yes. And don't try and wriggle your way into my will while you're down there! Because I've probably got cervical cancer haven't I? Well hopefully not, but I might. *(feels the insertion of the speculum)* THERE IT IS!
DR MAGDA:	Everything okay?
KATE:	Yep. You can really feel every little scrape of this thing can't you.
DR MAGDA:	*(finishing the procedure)* You can put your pants on now.

keys

KATE: I live with my brother Sammy. He's really getting into his cooking recently. He's decided to perfect one dish per week and this week it's Spaghetti Bolognese. I can't think about food unless I'm hammered at the moment. It's difficult to think about food when you're anxious isn't it? Anyway so in that respect, I'm really happy he's living with me because/

We hear **Sammy** *upstairs.*

SAMMY: FOR FUCK SAKE!
KATE: You what?
Sam?
Sammy!
SAMMY: What?
KATE: What?
SAMMY: What?
KATE: What's wrong?

SAMMY: What?
KATE: Just come downstairs I can't hear you!

Sammy *comes downstairs and is looking around for his keys.* **Kate** *is looking at him waiting for an answer.*

KATE: What's going on?

Sammy *stops and looks at* **Kate**.

SAMMY:	I'm looking for my keys.
KATE:	How many times do we have to go through this before you put them back in their spot.
SAMMY:	What spot?
KATE:	'The spot'. The spot which we spent a fucking week deciding on!
SAMMY:	*(mumbling)* Well clearly it wasn't a very good spot.
KATE:	What was that?
SAMMY:	Nothing.
KATE:	No, no, go on.
SAMMY:	Well clearly it wasn't a very good spot was it!
KATE:	No no no, do not even start! You're the one who said that the hallway was too obvious a place, and therefore a place you would never think of. Your fucking words Sam!
SAMMY:	*(impersonates Kate)* 'Your fucking words Sam.'
KATE:	Oh nice one you lemon'ead!

Kate *is embarrassed by the sheer lameness of her comeback.*

SAMMY:	*(leaving the room)* Lemon'ead? Oof nice. Really got me where it hurts there sis.
KATE:	Shut up! You know I struggle to think of insults on the spot!

Kate *is all wound up, she paces around angrily. She considers whacking a chair over in frustration.* **Sammy** *comes back into the room, he's found the keys.*

KATE: Coat pocket?
SAMMY: Coat pocket.
Sammy *is getting ready to leave.*
KATE: Wait I'm not going to be here when you get back coz I've got that work do.
SAMMY: Lucky you.
KATE: I know. Shoot me.
SAMMY: What's with the bean can?
KATE: I need to recycle it. I'll put it in the bin when I leave. But yeah so just leave my half of the spag on the side. And make sure that everything is easily visible and accessible for me to just put straight in the microwave coz I am getting fucked up tonight! Shot, shot, maybe a line, *(she impersonates snogging someone)*/
SAMMY: Where is it?
KATE: At some kind of old school cricket club, it's like half an hour on the bus.
SAMMY: You going to be alright?
KATE: Yeah course.
SAMMY: Getting there I mean.
KATE: Yes... I know what you meant. And yes I'll be fine. I've walked it through in my head and I've got my panic podcasts at the ready

	if I need! Also… I think sexy Gary is going to be there.
SAMMY:	Don't care. Right I'm off.
KATE:	Bye.
SAMMY:	Love you.
KATE:	Love you too dickhead.

Sammy *leaves.*

KATE:	Right. Let's do this Bitches!

Kate *picks up the can before she leaves.*

one two three drink

Music comes on. **Kate** *enters the cricket club. She has the bean can in her hand and pours herself a drink into it. She looks around as she anxiously quickly drinks from her can, she becomes drunk over the course of this next section.*

LINDA:	Kate! You came babe! Yey! How come you're so bloody late?
KATE:	I watched 7 buses come and go before I plucked up the courage to get on one.
LINDA:	Oh Kate! You are such a card! Still got your can of beans I see!
KATE:	Yeah, guess it's my thing now.
LINDA:	What are you like! Right, I'm off to boogie! Ey make sure you find me and Karen for when the Nolan Sisters come on! *(singing)* I'm in the mood for dancing… romancing…

Kate *watches* **Linda** *as she dances off.*

KATE:	Alright, work night out. Love it. Literally never been out with them before. Bet they all think it's fucking xmas. You're welcome! *(spots* **Sexy Gary***)* Oh… Sexy Gary is looking pretty sexy. Maybe tonight is the night I get more than three words out of him. Probably have to talk to him to

manage that… NAH! Just break out my best moves.

Kate *demonstrates her dance moves.*

KATE: Right, so first you wanna start with sexy, then a little funny, sexy again - 'wow she's sexy and she also has a sense of humour, what a find!'. Keep that up for a bit; Sexy. Funny. Sexy. Funny. Then, you wanna hit them with the 'I am also deep and have a lot of profound thoughts' look.

Kate *does the look.*

KATE: That should do it. Now look hot and head to the bar. Gary's hand should be making his way onto my back any minute/

Kate *acts out this next conversation as if Gary is talking to her.*

KATE: Y'alright Kate.
Gary? I didn't realise you were here tonight. You having a good night?
Yeah, all the better for seeing you dancing. Are you a professional?
Shut up!
No, I'm being deadly serious! I've never seen anything like it.

Oh well, thank you. Dancing makes me feel so free.

You looked a little away with your thoughts during the dance as well. Were you thinking about something… profound?

Oh… no I don't think… well, maybe? I just sometimes reflect on certain moments and think about how, in the grand scheme of things, we're all just so insignificant.

Wow. Kate.

Yes Gary?

I think… I think

Yes?

I think you could be the one…

Gary hasn't moved.

He's still by the bar. Talking to Melisa.

Kate *knows what she needs to do, she downs the remaining booze in her bean can and starts dancing attempting to grab* **Sexy Gary's** *attention.*

The booze has caught up with her, the music becomes louder and her tinnitus becomes unbearable. The ringing is invading her head. She tries to ignore it and keeps dancing. She feels self-conscious, a bit confused and scared. **Kate** *starts to experience derealisation. She feels disconnected from the world around her, or like the world isn't real. Everything slows down. The ringing continues. She grabs her bean can and leaves the cricket club.*

knitting

Kate *is at home, talking to herself.*

KATE: My lungs hurt. I'm going to die because of how much I smoked last night. End up in hospital with 5 months to live. With those tubes coming out of my neck. And then I'll die. I'll just be dead. I won't be able to think or laugh or continue. I'll just end.

Why does everything make me think about death?
I can't stop thinking about it. The release. I can't breathe I can't fucking breathe my head hurts. Stop it! Just… calm down.

Kate *remembers she has an audience.*

I like to do wholesome things after doing horrible stuff. Or when I've put my body through the mill. Makes me feel like I've pressed the reset button somehow. Sometimes, after a particularly disgusting sesh, I like to bake bread from scratch. Feels like it somehow balances out the filth.
This is it. New me. New leaf. New knickers. No more smoking, no more drinking. It's a raw vegan diet from here on out. Green

beans and broccoli. Jokes on you though because I actually love broccoli.

Do some sit ups. Alright that's enough. Water only. No coffee. No caffeine full stop. No butter on my toast, only hummus. And, for la piece de resistance... crafts!

Kate *goes to her laptop to search for a craft workshop.*

It's Saturday. There's definitely something going on somewhere. I live in a middle-class English town, they live for this shit. Ah yes! Perfect - beginners knitting workshop.

Kate *sets herself up for the knitting workshop. She brings her bean can with her.*

CLASS LEADER: You'll find your wool and needles in the drawers behind you, and be careful not to catch each other's nits. That was just a joke for everybody. Let's get knitting.

Kate *grabs her wool and needles, takes a seat, realises she's holding her bean can so slides it discreetly under her chair.*

CLASS LEADER: Right troupes! Needles in, yarn over, back through and off. Repeat. Needles in, yarn over, back through and off. Keep going!

Kate *is trying to follow with her knitting needles, looking around the room at the other workshop-goers.*

KATE: What the fuck. Okay. Insert, loop over, back… something… *(***Kate** *spots* **Shoe Man**.*)* Ooooo hello. He's a bit of alright in'e! I wonder what he's doing here? He's attractive. I bet he's wearing crocs. Let's just… *(***Kate** *drops her wool to check his shoes out under the table)* Nope, slightly dirty shoes of a person who understands that smoking is sexy and that's just a fact.

What is it then? Is he… *(he clocks eyes with* **Kate**, *she jerks her head away quickly)* Oh shit he's seen me.

Just concentrate on this. What even is this? A…scarf? Just look at that bitch over there. This is a beginners class. Ego-tripping maniac. She's nearly finished knitting herself a friend. Right okay. So, you put the stick in the back, you loop it over, and then the stick jumps over the other stick and then… you poke your fucking eyes out with it. This is supposed to be relaxing. Why am I even here? I could just buy myself a scarf. Absolute bullshit

Kate *finishes a row of knitting, she feels quite proud actually.*

> But guys to be fair… I did a row! *(to the ego-tripping maniac)* Yeah fuck you Mabel!
> Shoe man's noticed me.
> Game on.

Kate *picks up her bean can to use as a microphone, she becomes a commentator.*

> He's started off strong with a barely noticeable eye lift in my direction.
> *(Pause. Gaze down. eyelift!)* BOOM!
> Oof! That is a good first play from Shoe man. I can't come on too strong but can't be too subtle either. So I return with a classic but emphatic…
> *(Pause. Gaze in the opposite direction of* **Shoe man** *as if I'm day dreaming. Then flirtily whip head in his direction, fluttery eyes)* POW!
> Shoe man comes back straight away with the smile sniff!
> *(Smile sniff)* WHACK!
> He is good. Doesn't give me much choice really. This is it. Hero or Zero.
> *(Whip head to* **Shoe man,** *then bite lip to seal the deal)* KA BLAMO!

So I end up asking Shoe man out for a post-knit drink. I'm all like:
'Hey, wanna blow this cardigan-fest and grab a beer?'
He did. And we did. And. He's just so fucking boring. He keeps telling me how he feels about things. Like his thoughts and opinions about stuff that's happening in the world.

What really did it for me was when he got out a picture of his sister's new baby.

Kate *impersonates* **Shoe Man.**

'She's called Evelyn, oh I just love her. You know when you really love? The other day I was at hers, my sister's, she lives – actually! She doesn't live too far from here. You know where that old sweet shop used to be? Yeah well just round the corner from there. Basically, you just carry on in that same direction for roughly… 470 yards, and there's that right turning before the gold post box that takes you all the way down to Gradshore's Farm. Well it's not that right, it's actually the next left. And her house is the seventh from the bottom of the street with the bronze knocker. If you get to the house with the gnome collection, you've gone too far.'

I counter attack. Go in for the lean to shut him up.

He rejects me. So I take the baby photo that he's been wafting in my face, lick it, and drown it in my pint of local ale. Waste of a week's wages but worth it.

Shame he turned out to be so boring, I could have done with the distraction.

Having company just helps to shut up those little voices in your head at night. I don't really sleep.

I've had tinnitus in my right ear for six and a half weeks now. And when it's quiet, the constant ringing is just there reminding me that I'm trapped – in this body. And it could fail me at any moment.

I'm just not where I thought I would be. It's not how I pictured it.

So if I'm not sleeping, might as well have company!

Anyway Sammy was kind enough to leave me a goodnight joint by my bed. He never shares his weed so this was a big gesture. He's obviously heard me crying at night and this is his way of giving me a hug.

dyskari-what now?

Kate *approaches the GP surgery's reception, she's holding her bean can.*

KATE: Hello, oh...youagainHi.
RECEPTIONIST: Yes?
KATE: Good morning.
Receptionist *doesn't respond.*
KATE: Okay. Miss Kate Sharmack to see Doctor Magdalene Sweetbreads.
RECEPTIONIST: Doctor Magdalene Sniadek?
KATE: Oh yeah, yes. Yeah that sounds right.
RECEPTIONIST: Room 6.
Kate *goes into* **Dr Magda**'s *office and sits down.*
KATE: Good morning, how are you?
DR. MAGDA: Yes. So Kate, we have your results back from your smear test and you have high-grade dyskaryosis, otherwise known as severe cervical dysplasia. The next step is to book you in for a colposcopy where you will undergo a loop electrical excision procedure to prevent the cells progressing and leading to cancer.
KATE: I've got cancer.
DR MAGDA: No. There is a possibility that you have cancer, but that depends on the cells and whether they are cancerous or not.

KATE:	Right. So what you're saying is that I'm on amber when it comes to cancer. But it could turn to red or green? At the moment though, I don't have cancer.
DR MAGDA:	Well not exactly, we cannot categorically say that you are cancer-free.
KATE:	So I do have cancer.
DR MAGDA:	The colposcopy will help us determine whether the cells have the potential to turn cancerous.
KATE:	You are saying the word cancer a-lot though. And it's about me. Me and cancer. I'm used to cancer being paired with 'research' on the tele or on a charity shop sign. You've probably seen the adverts, they're on daytime TV a lot. Well actually you might not have seen them because you're probably at work when they're on. I pull a lot of sickies from work so I am sometimes at home during the week so I have seen them.
DR MAGDA:	Okay. So here's all the details for your colposcopy appointment. Is there anything else I can help you with?
KATE:	Yes… actually. I've been feeling a bit low recently, a bit grey and panicky. So for example the other night/

DR MAGDA:	Yes. We'll have to book you in for a double slot for this issue, see reception on the way out. Okay Kate? See you.
KATE:	Oh right. Out. Yes, see you…

outside

Kate *is outside the surgery with her bean can. She's trying to keep it together for her audience. Her tinnitus starts to get louder, her anxiety is building.*

Kate's *phone rings.* **Sammy** *is facetiming her. She answers.*

KATE:	What do you want Sam?
SAMMY:	Have you seen my keys?

Kate *deeply inhales, trying not to lose her absolute shit.*

KATE:	You do know that I'm not home don't you?
SAMMY:	Yeah.
KATE:	Then why would I know where your keys are?
SAMMY:	You know where they are when you're in a different room so why would being out of the house make any difference. You can't see them in either scenario.
KATE:	I'm not doing this right now Sam. I'm not feeling too great/
SAMMY:	Found them.
KATE:	Brilliant.
SAMMY:	Where are you?
KATE:	I've just come out of the doctors.
SAMMY:	Everything alright?

KATE:	I think I have cancer. I'm going to be dead in 5 years, I've looked it up and that's how long people usually last with cervical cancer.
SAMMY:	Wait. What? What are you talking about?
KATE:	My smear test came back and I have high-grade dyskarkikosis.
SAMMY:	Dyskariosis?
KATE:	Why do you know that word?
SAMMY:	What did the doctor say?
KATE:	I've got an operation on Thursday.
SAMMY:	That's a quick turnaround.
KATE:	Is it? Well, yeah I guess it is. They're probably trying to catch the cancer before it spreads anywhere else. But it probably already has. Why is this happening Sam?
SAMMY:	Listen, chill out, come home, I've made some lasagna.
KATE:	Why is it always pasta?
SAMMY:	You love pasta.
KATE:	I do.

colposcopy

Kate *is at the colposcopy clinic reception, bean can in hand - this is what she squeezes instead of* **Nurse**'s *hand.*

KATE: Hi, I have a colposcopy appointment. Kate Sharmack.

Kate *gets ready for the operation, wraps the medical tissue around her and gets into stirrups.*

NURSE: Alright love, so the doctor's ready to inject the local anaesthetic for you now. You might feel a slight scratching sensation. You're in good hands today Kate.
You alright my love?

Kate *nods and starts to cry.*

Yeah, oh sweetie, bless ya. Do you want to hold my hand?
KATE: Yes please.
NURSE: There you go. Oh it's a lot isn't it? You were probably nervous before coming here and it's all just coming out. You're doing really well Kate.
KATE: I'm just trying to be as relaxed as possible because I read that that helps.

NURSE: Yeah that's it, keep breathing. You got any plans for later on today? You got work or anything?

KATE: No, I'll probably just get stoned and go to the cinema with my brother. He's waiting for me outside.

NURSE: Aww that's brilliant. Well, listen afterwards we'll get you a nice cup of tea and some biscuits alright? And you can just sit for a bit, and your brother can come sit with you too. Does he drink tea?

The pain suddenly soars.

NURSE: Okay love, well done, that's the bad bit. We're almost done sweetheart. Almost there. You're alright.

What's your brother's name?

KATE: Sammy.

NURSE: That's nice of him to come with you isn't it? Have you always been close?

KATE: He's my favourite person.

Pain increases again.

NURSE: Deep breaths Kate.
There you go love. You're all done now. It's over.

saturday

Kate *is back at work.* **Annie** *goes past*

KATE:	Alright Annie. She stinks of fig rolls. *(spots* **Linda***)* Incoming.
LINDA:	Kate! Oh bloody hell I'm out of breath! Don't you get free coffees from the posh machine now?
KATE:	Oh my god. I totally forgot about that Linda. You know what, I could really do with one of those today/
LINDA:	It's broken! Oh Kate yeah, I doubt Chris'll fork out for another one of those do you? Tight git! BUT silver lining! Guess who's won the writing competition?

Kate *leans in with anticipation.*

	Me! I've only gone and bloody won it!
KATE:	Oh wow! That's excellent.
LINDA:	Oh no! You didn't enter it did you?
KATE:	Yeah but I didn't take it very seriously. I just quickly knocked something up and thought I might as well submit it you know. Congratulations anyway.
LINDA:	Oh thanks! Can't believe it! First thing I've ever written as well! Anyway just thought

> I'd tell you because we're pals ain't we! Don't want the whole office to know my business do I?! I'll see ya later!

We hear **Linda** *a few desks away.*

> Annie! You'll never guess what!

Kate *grabs her can for comfort, goes home and checks the letter box. A few letters in there, including one from the NHS. She shows it to her audience, she's nervous. Oh god, what if it's bad news.*

KATE: Just open it?

She opens the letter. It reads:
"Further to your visit to my colposcopy clinic, I have got the results of the lab tests performed on the biopsy taken from the neck of the womb. I am pleased to confirm that the abnormal cells appear to have been effectively treated at the same time. No further treatment is warranted. We will need to see you though at the nurses smear clinic in 6 months' time to assess the neck of the womb further with smears. A formal appointment will follow."

KATE: Oh thank fuck for that!

She grabs her phone to call **Sammy.**

SAMMY: Hello?

KATE:	Sam, I've got my results back. We're in the clear.
SAMMY:	What?
KATE:	I know! I was shitting myself when I was opening the letter but/
SAMMY:	No way!
KATE:	Yeah... what?
SAMMY:	Great. I can't actually hear you. This is my answer-machine. You know what to do
KATE:	You've got to change that it's doing my head in. Listen just call me back when you get this. K love you bye.

Kate *hangs up.*

What a wanker.

Kate's *relief turns into 'what ifs' in her head. Her tinnitus is getting very loud. No, why now? It's good, this is good news. She takes the letter, scrunches it up and shoves it in her bean can. She looks at her bean can for a moment. She's tired, she wants a break. She grabs her bean can and falls asleep holding it close to her on the floor.*
Tinnitus stops.

recycling

Kate *wakes up and checks her phone. She's late again. Grabs her bean can and goes to the GP Surgery.*

KATE:	Fucking hell. Why is it always the same receptionist?
	Hi there. Me again. Nothing huh? Okay. Miss/
RECEPTIONIST:	You're seeing Dr Twigden in room 3 Kate.
	…
	What?
KATE:	Nothing. Shall I just…?
RECEPTIONIST:	Yep.
KATE:	Always a pleasure.

Dr. Twigden's *room*.

DR. TWIGDEN: Hi Kate, come take a seat.

Kate *sits and puts her bean can down.*

DR. TWIGDEN: So Kate what can I do for you today?

KATE: I am sad.
I can see inside my body, I can see my brain breaking down or melting. I can see tumours in my ears. I get headaches all the

	time and I still have tinnitus in my right ear and I read that that's not normal and that it could be a sign of something more serious.
DR. TWIGDEN:	Like a tumour?
KATE:	Yeah.
DR. TWIGDEN:	Alright.
KATE:	I know that what I'm saying sounds irrational. And that it's all probably just in my head, but to me it's real. I really see inside my body. I can really see it. I'm frightened to close my eyes at night because I'm convinced I'm going to wake up blind. Since the tinnitus started, I've been waiting to go deaf. I'm so stressed out. I can't think about anything else because any little minor ache or pain anywhere makes me feel like I'm being given a slow death sentence. I got a letter saying that my operation was successful and that the biopsy showed no cancerous cells. But what if it comes back and I die? I think about death all the time. I can't stop thinking about it. What it'll feel like. I really don't want to die. I'm so scared. All the time.
DR. TWIGDEN:	Well let's take one thing at a time okay? I'm going to check your ears now. Okay, Kate, if you turn to your right please.

That's your left.

And to your left.

Yep, they look perfectly healthy. Very healthy ears Kate.
I think that in this case, it's more the stress that we need to look at managing rather than there being anything physically wrong with your ears.

Kate, just so you everything that you say in this room is confidential. I just need to know if you've had any thoughts about hurting yourself or others?

KATE: No.

DR. TWIGDEN: Any suicidal thoughts?

KATE: I don't want to die but if I was dead I wouldn't have to worry about dying.

DR. TWIGDEN: Kate I'm going to refer you to a service in the local area, which'll offer you 6 counselling sessions initially. But if you say anything in those sessions that indicates you need more help - they will be able to refer you to a psychiatrist. In the meantime, here are some phone numbers you can call if you feel like it's all getting too much.
Is that alright?

KATE:	Yes.
DR. TWIGDEN:	Apart from that, making sure you look after yourself, getting enough sleep, you know, exercise helps a lot of people who suffer with stress. And you can always call the surgery and make an appointment to come and see us if you need.
KATE:	Okay, thanks.

Kate *starts to leave, she leaves her bean can.*

DR. TWIGDEN:	Take care.
KATE:	Bye.

Kate *starts to leave, but realises that she's forgotten the bean can.*

KATE:	Oh bollocks, *(comes back and picks up the bean can)* my can.
DR. TWIGDEN:	Out of interest, why do you have an empty can of beans with you?
KATE:	I just keep forgetting to put it in the bin.
DR. TWIGDEN:	I can throw it away for you if you like?
KATE:	Oh no, no I mean I'm trying to recycle it sorry. I'm sure I'll find the right bin. Eventually.
DR. TWIGDEN:	We've got one.
Kate:	Yeah, I'm pretty serious about recycling it you know – I don't want it to just go in the bin. To be honest, I don't even know what

                  bin it's supposed to go in. I mean can you put this bit *(the can lid)* inside or will that cause some sort of congestion? And this bit *(the ring pull)*, the lip bit, is that fine to be recycled or is it like bottle lids? Or can they be recycled now?

                  It's a bit confusing.

                  It's a fucking nightmare actually.

DR. TWIGDEN: Yeah we have the right bins. I'm also a fascist recycler. I'll sort it for you, don't worry.

Kate *considers the offer before handing the bean can over to* **Dr. Twigden**, *letting it go and accepting the help.*

KATE: Thank-you.

The end.

PROCRASTINATION

- When I went to have the actual colposcopy done. I cried. It'd be good to capture that. Overwhelming emotion.
- Then told to come back again
- Getting that letter. Feeling okay then just really not. The finality.?

- <u>Recycling</u> - oh god I really should find a recycling bin → what about at the start of the performance she has a bottle and she is like oh no I'm going to recycle it and then she just ends up carrying it everywhere because she keeps forgetting to put it into recycling.

"Shall I throw this away for you?"
"Oh no that's fine I'm going to recycle it and we don't have a recycle bin here do we?" [Jo: coz we apparently live in the middle of fucking Sudan.]

"Why are you carrying an empty can of soup/baked beans/ Hula hoops / with you?"

Damn it!

Before this - talk about needing help.
think about death.

End: "Hey." "Yeah." "I can throw that away for you."

I'm just really scared.

closing my eyes feeling like I'm going blind. scared I'm going

P.T.O. to lose my hearing.

wittering.

"Oh no I'm trying to recycle it thanks. I'll just find a bin when I leave."
"We've got one."
"One what? A bin? Yeah, I mean a recycling bin. To be honest I don't even know what bin it's supposed to go in. I mean does the top go in a seperate bin. And what about this bit. [The bit of plastic attached to a carton.] I mean I'm pretty sure this is for the Blue Bin but do I cut this bit off? It's a fucking nightmare to be honest mate. I mean Doctor. I mean Mr Twigden. Sorry."

"Yeah we have the right bins. We recycle. I'll sort it for you." → exhausted
Thank-you
The end. (LoL)

- Colposcopy, Loop incision + initial smear test. Good or Bad to have 5 legs in stirrups scenes? Good to show how often ladies find themselves in these positions.

- It's a love letter to my girls + boys. Your stories help my days.

- Definitely a funny bit with me @ gym - Kettlebells, spinning (add on!) (add on!) 'faster' - come on!